WORLD'S
FASTEST
DINOSAURS

Rupert Matthews

Heinemann Library
Chicago, Illinois

www.capstonepub.com
Visit our website to find out more information about Heinemann-Raintree books.

To order:
☎ Phone 888-454-2279
▣ Visit www.capstonepub.com to browse our catalog and order online.

© 2012 Heinemann Library
an imprint of Capstone Global Library, LLC
Chicago, Illinois

Edited by Rebecca Rissman and Laura Knowles
Designed by Richard Parker
Picture research by Mica Brancic
Originated by Capstone Global Library Ltd
Printed and bound in China by CTPS

15 14 13 12 11
10 9 8 7 6 5 4 3 2 1

Library of Congress Cataloging-in-Publication Data
Matthews, Rupert.
World's fastest dinosaurs / Rupert Matthews.
   p. cm.—(Extreme dinosaurs)
Includes bibliographical references and index.
ISBN 978-1-4109-4524-2 (hb)—ISBN 978-1-4109-4531-0 (pb) 1. Dinosaurs—Juvenile literature. I. Title.
QE861.5.M3745 2012
567.9—dc23   2011016098

Acknowledgments
We would like to thank the following for permission to reproduce images: © Capstone Publishers pp. **4** (James Field), **5** (Steve Weston), **6** (Steve Weston), **7** (Steve Weston), **8** (James Field), **10** (James Field), **11** (James Field), **12** (James Field), **13** (Steve Weston), **14** (James Field), **16** (Steve Weston), **17** (James Field), **18** (Steve Weston), **19** (James Field), **20** (James Field), **21** (James Field), **22** (Steve Weston), **23** (James Field), **24** (James Field), **25** (Steve Weston), **26** (James Field), **27** (Steve Weston); © Miles Kelly Publishing p. **15** (Kevin Maddison); Shutterstock p. **29** (© Paul B. Moore).

Background design features reproduced with permission of Shutterstock/© Szefei/© Fedorov Oleksiy/© Oleg Golovnev/© Nuttakit.

Cover image of a *Gallimimus* reproduced with permission of © Capstone Publishers/James Field.

We would like to thank Nathan Smith for his invaluable help in the preparation of this book.

Contents

Some words are shown in bold, **like this**.
You can find out what they mean by
looking in the glossary.

Super Speedsters

Not all **dinosaurs** were big and slow. Some were very fast! Being able to run quickly allows hunters to catch **prey**. But being fast also helps prey to escape hunters! The plant-eating dinosaur *Orodromeus* used its speed to escape from hunters such as *Troodon*.

Troodon

Orodromeus

Dawn Thief

The hunter *Eoraptor* was one of the earliest **dinosaurs**. It lived about 230 million years ago. *Eoraptor* was around 3 feet long. That's about the size of a dog.

Eoraptor used its speed to hunt small lizards and **mammal**-like animals. Its front legs were short, with claws that were used to grab **prey**. *Eoraptor* could then eat its food as it ran along!

Eoraptor

Did You Know?
Eoraptor's name
means "dawn thief."

Ready for Action

Animals that run fast need to keep their muscles warm so that they are ready for instant action. Scientists think that fast **dinosaurs** such as *Gallimimus* were covered in short, narrow feathers. These helped to keep the animal warm. *Gallimimus* could run about 35 miles per hour. That's faster than a giraffe can run!

Did You Know?

Gallimimus had hollow bones. Its light bones probably helped it to run fast.

Gallimimus

The Terrible Claws

Deinocheirus had massive claws almost 10 inches long on the end of arms more than 8 feet long. Only the arms and claws of this **dinosaur** have been found. Scientists think *Deinocheirus* was about 23 feet long— more than half as long as a bus! But it could still run nearly 31 miles per hour.

The Fastest of Them All

The **dinosaur** *Struthiomimus* was one of the fastest dinosaurs of all. It could run almost 45 miles per hour. That is faster than the speed limit for most town and city streets! The dinosaur's long legs were powered by massive muscles around its hips.

13

Sky Swooper

Pterosaurs were flying **reptiles** that had bodies covered in fur to help keep their muscles warm. Early types such as *Rhamphorhynchus* had a long tail. They could swoop down to catch fish or insects. The long, thin wings of later pterosaurs meant that they could travel long distances by gliding on the wind.

Rhamphorhynchus

Speedy Thief

The hunting **dinosaur** *Velociraptor* has a name that means "speedy thief." It could run quickly to catch **prey** such as *Protoceratops*. Then it used the large, curved claw on its back foot to kill. Two or more *Velociraptors* may have worked together when hunting.

Twilight Hunter

Anserimimus's huge eyes helped it to see in the dark. It probably sped around in the dark, catching fast insects and small animals. *Zephyrosaurus* had short, deep jaws that were probably used to crunch up tough plants. It used its long, powerful back legs to run away from hunters.

Zephyrosaurus

Anserimimus

19

Forest Runner

Ornithomimus was almost 12 feet long, the length of a small car! But it weighed only about 119 pounds, which is less than an adult human. It was a slim animal that could run quickly. It used its tail as a weight to hold its body steady. This meant it could change direction suddenly— even when running at full speed!

Ornithomimus

Speeding to Space

Coelophysis was a slim, swift animal about 10 feet long. Scientists have found groups of *Coelophysis* that all died together in a flood. This **dinosaur** may have hunted in family groups. The climate in **Triassic** times was dry, so *Coelophysis* probably sped across dry plains and deserts hunting for lizards and other small animals.

Coelophysis

Did You Know?

A *Coelophysis* skull was taken into space by the Space Shuttle *Endeavour* on January 22, 1998.

Heterodontosaurus

Heterodontosaurus was a small plant eater. The bones of its back feet were joined together. This gave the **dinosaur** extra strength when it was running at full speed to escape from hunters.

Another speedy plant eater was *Leaellynasaura* from Australia. *Leaellynasaura* was more than 6 feet long.

Leaellynasaura

Heterodontosaurus

25

Nest of Killers

Troodon was a small, speedy hunter that lived about 70 million years ago in North America. In 1983 **fossilized** nests with *Troodon* eggs were found in the state of Montana. It is thought that one parent sat on the eggs to keep them warm, while the other hunted for food.

Troodon

Where Are Fossils Found?

Scientists who study **dinosaurs** are called paleontologists. Paleontologists know about dinosaurs from studying **fossils**. Scientists have to travel all over the world to find dinosaur fossils.

Sometimes the fossils are in deserts hundreds of miles from the nearest road. Sometimes the fossils are in back gardens or on farmland. A scientist may have to search for weeks before he or she finds a fossil. But sometimes a fossil is found right next to where the scientist has parked the car!

Glossary

dinosaur group of animals that lived on land millions of years ago during the Mesozoic Era

fossil part of a plant or animal that has been buried in rocks for millions of years

fossilized when something becomes a fossil

mammal warm-blooded animal covered in fur. The mother feeds her babies with her own milk.

prey animal that is eaten by another animal

pterosaurs group of flying reptiles that lived between 220 and 65 million years ago

reptiles cold-blooded animals such as lizards or crocodiles

Triassic period in Earth's history that began about 250 million years ago and ended about 200 million years ago

Find Out More

Books

Bingham, Caroline. *Dinosaur Encyclopedia.* New York: Dorling
    Kindersley, 2009.

Lessem, Don. *The Ultimate Dinopedia.* Washington, DC: National
    Geographic Children's Books, 2010.

Markarian, Margie. *Who Cleans Dinosaur Bones?* Chicago:
    Heinemann-Raintree, 2010.

Matthews, Rupert. *Ripley Twists: Dinosaurs.* Orlando, FL: Ripley
    Publishing, 2010.

Websites

science.nationalgeographic.com/science/prehistoric-world.html
Learn more about dinosaurs and other facts about the prehistoric
world at this National Geographic Website.

www.ucmp.berkeley.edu/
Learn more about fossils, prehistoric times, and paleontology
at this Website of the University of California Museum of
Paleontology.

www.nhm.ac.uk/kids-only/dinosaurs
The Natural History Museum is located in London, England. Its
Website has a lot of information about dinosaurs, including facts,
quizzes, and games.

www.kidsdinos.com/
Play dinosaur games and read about dinosaurs on this Website.

Index